ℛEMYTH

A POSTMODERNIST RITUAL

REMYTH

A POSTMODERNIST RITUAL

ADAM D. MARTINEZ

Inlandia Books

Cover, book design, and layout: Kenji C. Liu

Printed and bound in the United States
Distributed by Ingram

Published by Inlandia Institute
Riverside, California
www.InlandiaInstitute.org
First Edition

For Adam, before he found cognitive behavioral therapy.
For Mago, the hardworking grandfather of a published poet.
For my ancestors in my own small way.
For the America I grew up in.
For all seekers among wolves.

CONTENTS

III: SACRED MYSTERY SONGS

IV: ENDNOTES

V: AUTHOR'S NOTE

VI: ACKNOWLEDGMENTS

I. BEDLAM

"Your vision will become clear only when you can look into your own heart. Who looks outside dreams; who looks inside, awakens."

— CARL GUSTAV JUNG

BUILD

WALK into the river until you can't touch the bottom without baptism. Rocks in your pocket will hold you down. The past is a wilderness of horrors. Build a house for the dead to live in. Count crows' feet out of the corner of your eye. Souls meet at high tide where waves crash on cliff sides. Low tide invites you, "come inside." In the ocean, life and death converge and all we love we leave behind.

IN THE JUNGLE OF my mind I penetrate provenance with the passion of a lover hacking at wild vines. Creating thousands of cuts so clean that I never feel a thing. I bleed language. I see double in the junkyard of my mind. Jumbled lies and lives lie in rubble. Make sense of the wreckage. Colonize you—self-appropriation. Tear trees from roots and children from the womb. Man eating fellow man. Descending into barbarism. It begins at home.

REPRESSION keeps us safe but dare to shake the foundation. Peel that second layer. Floating spit hovering, holding my mood in with every word I choose not to say. Moments of sheer panic, aching for who we were like missing your gall bladder when it's removed. It's beautiful organ donor weather. My death is your holiday. I left my body for you, ask the paramedics for my driver's license. Scrape me off of this newly constructed highway. Sun, shine on this somnambulist. The self is split. Destroy and rebuild destroy and rebuild destroyandrebuild.

WITHOUT LANGUAGE

Drought on the tongue
Dehydrated dialogue
Without water flowing
From a stream-of-consciousness

My ideology
Is incomplete as is
Insult without apology
Remorse without forgiveness

What is man without
God
Or a god without
Man?

Existing in the imaginary
Afraid to carry a conversation
The victim in us
The fear of criticism

Words become worthless
Diction with broken wings
Ideas with no place to go
Vagabond vocabulary

Without pretensions or agendas
No preaching atop a soapbox
No makeshift pulpit to wash your mouth of sins
Without pressure I'll understand if you walk away

Speak without restraint
Speak slowly
Speak today without tomorrow
Dear Language,
        I am not my-Self without you.

SCAREHEAD

l am the pill. l am the noose.
l am all the rage.
l can make front page.
l am the shooting.

l am the victim of a television
murder mystery.
l am an icon. l am a god.
l am Kanye's unrestrained ego.

l am a cultural phenomenon.
l am Heisenberg.
l cut the blue sky.
l defy cancer—twice.

l am the various bombings
    in red and blue states.
l am Columbine and the like.
l am September 11th.

l am Rodney King's beating;
l am a subsequent riot.
l am post-Katrina New Orleans.
l am a high-speed chase

    involving a Chicano male, 18-24,
    involved in a robbery.
l am the unsolved murder
    of Christopher Wallace and Tupac Shakur.

l am the O.J. trial.
l am Trayvon Martin.
l am Jon-Benét Ramsay.
l am the Menendez Brothers.

I am the advent of the talk show.
I am a Hip-Hop vixen's tell-all.
I am reality T.V.
I am my own enterprise.

I am the walking dead.
I have a virus. I am a virus.
I belong in a virtual mass grave.
I am the news and I'm happening so fast.

DEATH AT THE LOG-IN SCREEN

I am a victim of the digital age.
I am the time America went online.
I am aggregated data.
I am a username.

I am nothing more than
    a broken-hearted hashtag.
I never stop to smell the roses
I bite my tongue.

    It tastes like
    what it means
    to be
    an American.

    You get what you ask for:
    Information at break-neck speeds.
I am dada.
    Well beyond Futurism.

    Well beyond our means.
I want to become extinct
    on the internet
    vanish into static.

INSTITUTIONS OF FUCKERY (LIST INCOMPLETE):

American public school systems,
universities,
student loans,
fraternities and sororities,
Wal-Mart, McDonalds,
and liquor stores,
Sureños, Bloods and Crips,
NBA, NFL, and MLB,
Nightclubs, gastropubs,
and strip clubs,
the porn industry,
prisons and police departments,
Big 4 banks—Bank of America,
Chase, Citi and Wells Fargo,
Big 4 record labels—Universal Music Group,
Sony BMG, EMI and Warner Music Group,
Clear Channel Radio,
Worldstar,
TMZ, Hollywood,
high-end fashion, reality TV,
the US government,
it goes on...

REVOLUTIONARY MUSIC THROUGH A WHITE MALE GAZE

To profit from your disgrace,
we watch your music videos
in which you're
popping bottles.

We keep the corks,
pour alcohol over them,
light matches and
burn them to a crisp.

We mash the ash into powder
and add water.
We stir into a thick paste,
now we wear your face!

Making money off of
painting vulgar pictures.
Somewhere in the USA,
a white girl is twerking.

Every privileged hipster loves to slum
with the new punks.
"Everybody wanna be a n—,
but don't nobody wanna be a n—."

Adopt the language
but can't adopt the anguish,
cultural rapists
with 'phat' pockets.

I pray to be currency
of cultural exchange.
I pray to stay current
and take over the game.

NANCY CALLAHAN DATES A RAPPER

you take it in
stride with

style and grace
ripped right out of me

my rib
my sin

my fruit of knowledge
belabored by your work

Every lackadaisical cumshot.
Every misogynistic monosyllabic word
Is for every girl to get drunk and dance to.

Let me participate in your experience.
Paint me purple and blue beaten
Barely breathing.

Maybe I will let you drive us home—
Sweet Skinny Callahan, stop the car, confirm the kill.
Come, make sure you shot him right between the eyes.

"'Dear Mama' by 2Pac is playing on the radio.
My mother is a woman. I should have thought of that
Before I called you a bitch."

CLOSE YOUR EYES

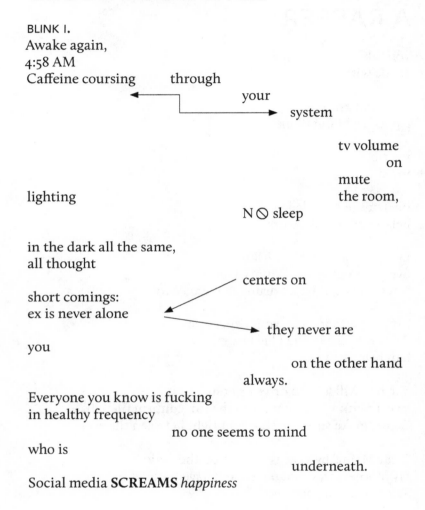

BLINK I.
Awake again,
4:58 AM
Caffeine coursing   through
your
system

tv volume
on
mute
lighting   the room,
N ⊘ sleep

in the dark all the same,
all thought

centers on
short comings:
ex is never alone
they never are
you
on the other hand
always.
Everyone you know is fucking
in healthy frequency
no one seems to mind
who is
underneath.
Social media **SCREAMS** *happiness*

I can't have anything to myself
not a single solitary thing

favorite: food   band   book   movie
        beer   sports team   city
      belongs to another name on the screen

someone else   already owns
your identity   &   plays the
role better
     all of your friends are assholes
   every + body = self-righteous poser
    the   world is   a   cunt

BLINK III.
oneday you woke up angry at the world and now
you're scared of sleep because you have to wake up
and do it all over all over all over allover alloverallover

every + one = opinionated fuck
      too much time on hand
      but not more than you
         you are a master of lost hours
      self-deprecation
  has become
your greatest hobby

BLINK IV.
You scroll through your networks and notice your friend's
status has changed to "engaged" you leave a congratulatory
comment when really you want to unsubscribe, burning.

There will be a wedding invitation in the mail. Another
for a baby shower with a picture of your old friend and his
fiancée glowing full-bellied. You probably won't go to either
    Maybe the wedding, only if you can find someone to sleep
with after free dinner, open bar and dancing
    You scroll through contacts for potentials and get
distracted reading pop culture headlines diatribes junk info-
dump.

BLINK V.
you concentrate on
the worst moments
in your past the most heinous things
that you had control over

                                        this is the closest
                                    you will ever come
                                            to suicide
                                            you need
                                to write this all down

            or
                    it.
                            will.
                                kill.
                                    you.

BLINK VI.
You are the pretentious writer
wielding his diction
in all of its phallic glory
You think
fuck him
the waxing and waning
go to sleep
You think

You hear your neighbor get in her car and start it around 5 AM.
You want to tell her shut up

you're trying to sleep deep down you're glad she's there
you feel less alone.

BLINK VII.
Count sheep   I...2...3...
Pills to sleep   4...5...6...
woe-is-me   ☹
The ability to feel is   key.

panicky breath &
w   i   d   ee   y   e   s.
You can't turn it off.
The motor runs.
Neurons or whatever
the fuck
they're called

driving

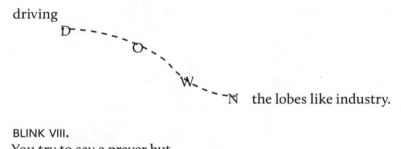 the lobes like industry.

BLINK VIII.
You try to say a prayer but
can't concentrate
You feel guilty
You used to be able to pray yourself to sleep
You miss sleeping next to her
Her blood always kept you warm

You still left the TV on.

She would always fall asleep before you. You held her
                              held her full breasts.
Or sometimes she would rest her head in the nape of your neck.
Whoever said, "sleep is for the weak" is full of shit.
You try once more: "Dear God..."

l dreamt a dream
that dragged me
          d
          o
          w
          n
                    WAY
                              d

                         o

               w

          n
               like a drug came creeping   back in my brain
i felt like   **NOTHING**
a waste of space
          taking up air
                    wishing the earth would swallow me whole

want to live *la vie en rose*
life in a rosy hue
          life through rose-colored glasses
place two petals in
                    the shallow holes where my eyes were
                                             leave me.

THE MEANING OF A GNAT

Every body
has a meaning.
For example, a
gnat. Annoying,
little thing.

Why are you alive?
To pester me and
my murderous desire.
Who will keep you safe?
Who will let you live?
I will swat you down
and let your guts stick
to the crumb-stricken counter

and an old newspaper in
a suffocating
apartment, all because you
won't leave me be while
I search for a glass
to fill with whiskey
because I really
have nothing going for me.

Heed my warning,
you mosquito,
sucking me dry
in the dead night,
you roach encroaching
under the fridge,
I want your scum
splayed about abundantly.

ENNUI

Today
At work
My thumb
Paper cut
So today
All I
Drank was
Blood

Yesterday
I didn't eat
I only drank
Black Sumatra
At work
I pissed
The scent

For lunch
I murdered
A spider that
Crawled across
My cubicle
Life's a Penny
Dreadful

Tomorrow
At work
It will be
The same
Blood and piss
And innards
Confined
And flooded

In a week
Or a month

Or a year
If you find
My body here
I was
Murdered by
Monotony

I TURNED ON
THE TELEVANGELISM

I turned on the television,
half-drunk.
The cable box was left on
the bible channel.

> The wife of
> a famous televangelist
> held a bouquet of daisies
> in a white wedding gown.

She stood
on a cliff-side meadow
overlooking the ocean,
pleading with me:

> *Jesus, the man born in Jerusalem,*
> as she pointed to her left
> as if he were standing off-screen
> *suffered for* me, *the proverbial sinner.*

I already believed her
so I changed the channel,
surfing until I found
a rerun of *Breaking Bad*.

HIGH ON RECYCLED AIR

People-watching in terminals.
Drinking coffee. Finally,
aboard. Shutting off
all electronics devices.
Safety routine as
a wave of
panic rushes over.
Ascension akin to
climbing tracks on
a coaster. However,
no drop is
anticipated, nor wanted.
Thinking of nose-diving
is dizzying. Fear
of deep vein
thrombosis. Fear of
the monster on
the wing. Fear of 9/11. Fear
of engine falling
in a vortex
and landing in
Donnie Darko's room.
Gasping for some
shared recycled air.
Rippling white sheets
mountains clumps of
mud. God is
a child playing
with cars, building
intricate cities, suburbs
as alien as
crop circle designs.
We live under
menacing demons, lions,
Chinese imperial dragons
spitting thunder-fire.

Greek myths hurdling
lightning at the
innocent. Winged-beasts
populate the sky
There are no
angels in heaven.
"Have a safe flight."

A GUIDE TO SURVIVING THREE DAYS IN THE DESERT

Find a plot of land
Roll in grass
Don't sleep too long

Elongate your loins
Brush crust from eyes
Relieve yourself

Splash water
Anoint yourself
in appropriation

The Haus of the Sun
(Hipsterdom)
The desert is burning alive

Sunburn
Sweat in your eyes
Bruise and blister

Dust in your nose
All night you're like a moth
Drawn to light

If you want to feel *something*
Ingest until you feel *nothing*
Magical realism

Carry cute little zip-locks
(jointswithhash, prescription pills, mushrooms, mollies, coke and x)
Spirograph a head spin

Follow the tesla claw
To feel safe in a strange oasis
Go to bed with someone

And wake up in love
Leave a part of you behind
Those dusty worried shoes

The grime of this world
Let someone fathom
The road you traveled

PERFUMED APOCALYPSE

10

Reading perfumed magazines
in white-walled waiting rooms.
Holding sterilized hands,
our love is cold and clinical.

9

Watching the world burn
in celluloid dreams.
Technicolored collisions between
our w s o d r l l r d o s w until
earth implodes.

8   We witness
chaos and fragmentations
sitting on decrepit rooftops
under Milky Way skylines.

7

Inside of you like a bullet in a gun,
safety off while the world falls apart.
Morbid romantics dancing into
post-war emptiness
in a field of *Harold and Maude* sunflowers
on a pulverized planet.
Every day at war with the sun—
Paint the world a postmodern gray.

6

Learning of death through
brief sentences.
Do you see? How fast? News travels.
How fast.   It comes and goes.
Jetting archers' arrows, straight through
the apple of my eye. Playing William Tell
with compassionate hearts.
Finding love in hopeless places
where marksmen take shots
at random targets,

5

a roaming photographer
at a downtown discothèque
overdoes it. Angel dusted.
Overdosed. Angel lust.
Rigamortis orgies
in memoriam of
lost angels in Los Angeles.
Kissing corpses, sacred and profane.
My lips meet the perverse imp's—
Color-coded in postmodern grays.

4

Collapsing and condensing all collected hate
into a twinkling of unadulterated violence.
The darker the news, the grander the narrative.
The author becomes the terrorist.

3
Life is TV
Who killed Laura Palmer?
Sad lives satirized,
gallows humor—
it's funny in a sick way,
in a fucked up way.

2
All of life is a burning house.
We relocate inside a textbox.
I want to live a literary life,
in a pre-war apartment.
For now, I'm fine with falling
for girls in magazine ads

1
because reality bites—
Chewed to bits, I am postmodern gray matter.

II. HYPER-VIOLENT
ROMANTICISM

"The heart was made to be broken."

— OSCAR WILDE

BROKEN BALLERINA

fuck grammar
i appreciate
you human
full of
error mistakes
so succinct
in sync-
opated rhythm
fluid and
frequent like
a *plié*
mimic
ballet
something
similar
to *meiple*
gaze at
body move
elegantly gallant
until time falls out of joint

like a knee
the tongue
is twisted
writhing with
heinous writing
ankle sprained
iridescent
idiomatics
dance inside
the mind with
arabesque
intentions
phrases *pirouette*
a meticulous
mise-en-scène
everything in
front of
us is microbotic
spell-check
sterilized
language
prancing
pretty
in perfect
punctuation
instead
making
money
taking off
tutus to
show off
every blemish
on our
bodies
because
propriety is so
passé

NYE13

at midnight
you walk up to me
I run my lips into yours
I think you hate me
a week before
you didn't reply to my texts
but I waited   and   I waited
do you want me or not
acid in system
pretty little sedated you
you whisper
I want you
you little troublemaker you
little death
you undertaker
I'm buried

Little DEATH

Treat me like a lady lay waste to me like the land for imperial taking Now Gentrify me rape me to rest For I am something new Help me and Heal me With feeling Conclude me My killing Decisively die Climax To deny In crisis These Dive in devices Divisively Dividing me Fill me Come inside and Fuck and Come alive Fulfill me that means Whatever. Gay me (empty erotic rhetoric)

BREAK

In the spring time,
as you exit the bounce house,
you slip and fall to the grass
just a few feet below.

    A bone bursts up
    in your right wrist
    and your hand stretches
    stiffly like a flower's bloom.

        It is bro-
            ken and
        the party is over
        before it began.

In the winter
you wake up
when you hear
the coffee-maker

    buzz,
        ready.

You reach for
your phone and
read a text:
"I wish

    I hadn't
    slept with you."
    This is how you
    break news.

You break a line
like this.
Now, I am on a different line.

The phone call is on hold.

You break a line when your brain needs to breathe or your
lungs lose logic.

ON WEEKENDS

I am a TV set
left on in an
empty room.

When the bar
closes, we split
a six-pack

a freshly rolled joint
and a pocket full
of horses.

So you go
through the motions
and you finally arrive.

The party is over
and you realize
you didn't want to party.

It simply sounded
like a sound idea
at the time.

Drunk and stoned.
In this bed
with any body again.

Listening to
Janet Jackson's
"Again".

Lovely, lonely life,
what's one more day without love?
Loyal to nothing that lives

I drive home
low on gas
and think.

ALIENATED INTELLECTUALS
AND SUICIDAL YOUTH

Leaving Soda Bar,
it's wet and mist stabs
at your windows.
There is constant threat
of hydroplaning.
The world becomes
a wrecking ball.
Driving in fog;
midnight marine layer.
It makes you want
to be moral.
You pop in an old mix
you made in college.
You called it
Guardian of an Infinite Abyss
It's been nine years
since you were 18 –
you drive a little safer now.

Sometimes you gotta let go,
close your eyes and let it crash.
Ignoring the
engine check light
after an evening
with Clarimonde.
You think you've found some-
one worth a damn,
You just haven't earned it yet baby,
you must suffer and cry for a longer time.
Until then,
fucking in bathroom stalls,
the smell of rotting flowers,
delight the delicate
dilettantes.

White linen faces,
little ghosts in
natural colors.
Haunted cones and rods.
Antagonized by what drips
down your throat.

Regardless of weather,
you wear your heart
on your sleeveless
roadkill overcoats.

IT HAPPENS ALL THE TIME

"It's not fair to you."
The oldest trick in the book,
as if it absolves you
from administering
a Milgram shock
to my system.

[dream sequence]
My teeth falling out
in a field of daisies.
I see my first lover
for the first time in years
wearing a daisy chain on her head,
the white petals red.

I tried my best
to forget your favorite songs.
You left your skin behind,
strands of your hair
on my pillowcase.
All the while, I'm on your body—
those tattoos about me.

DRESSER DRAWERS

At the
      bottom
of my dresser drawer

                  themiddlerow

where I keep dark colored t-shirts
black and blue
I still have
that   one shirt
of that   one band
            we watched
at that   one show
that   one time
on Sunset
seven or eight years

                       behind us

folded neatly
I no longer wear it

                 I no longer listen

Topleft
dresser drawer
unused
rubbers
from wrecked relationships
used to stroke waves
with shipmates lost at sea
the clean up is easier
than lotion and tissues
filled with shame and regret
lying next to my bed.
We lied   a couple   of times
                       BUT

other   than   that
                 bed
we   have   not
         a   thread of commonality
save   for   that   thread count

Into the   l a t e xa   b   y   s   s
millions of myself leave

                                        exit my body
                                            /

vanish immediately—   obsolete orphans die exactly
                              in the oxygen offered
                              above
                                    the mess of my potential
puddled in the comfort of my lonely queen bed.

EMILY WAS THE BROKEN ONE

Her voice fell

out of tune:

a few screws loose that
I never tightened up again.

After being left alone in your hallway
for days, she became more

hollow

than before with a

sunburnt body

but always indoors with
fingers and palms
sweating around her neck.

Plucking at your heart strings,

black around the edges,

I let you keep her
so that you might remember

the times that I played you
"Play Crack the Sky" and

"Everlong".

You always loved that song.

MOZ KNOWS

Steven Patrick Morrissey
swings a bundle of yellow
gladioli, lamenting
a charming man.

Pulls them from his back pocket
and flings them into the crowd.
Women swoon. Men swoon
for the boy with a thorn in his side.

This process repeats itself
as I press play on the video player.
Learning a little more about love lost,
Please, please, please, let me get what I want.

Praying for a postmodern pompadour,
one ripe with repression and
supernatural power. Unfortunately,
my hairdresser is on fire.

AN EXORCISM

I Lysol your lipstick
off of my coffee mug
and remove the movies
you added to my list

Possessions possess me
I want my fucking book back
Less Than Zero
my tie too
black and thin
like your persona

Take back your book
Heart of Darkness
and that picture of us
I left in the front cover

There is no room
at the Ace Hotel
no doo-wop in the desert
yet I dance alone with ghosts

YELLOW BUG

Floral arrangement class
at the adult ed:
Mom made a new friend.
We walked to the park
and sat on the swing set.
Me, Mom and him.

The man who drove the yellow Bug,
he wrecked our happy home.

One night I woke up alone
in the room we shared.
Dad picked up when I rang.
Mother and
neighbor.
Father hit mother. Cops on Christmas Eve.

The man who drove the yellow Bug,
he wrecked our happy home.

Mom went to the E.R.
I waited for Santa Claus.
With a broken nose,
she watched me
open gifts
on Christmas morn. Dad was gone because

the man who drove the yellow Bug,
he wrecked our happy home.

Faithfulness
escapes from the yard
like a runaway dog.
Infidelity is
in me like
sitting in that

yellow Bug
that wrecked our happy home.

GENEVIEVE STREET

On early evenings, a woman and her son would
walk several blocks to buy groceries. Food stamps
kept him fed a few times. Passing streetlights with a
tangerine glow, the fire station to the right, an empty
elementary on the left. Trees with low-hanging leaves
and shoes tangled in power lines, housing project
apartment complexes. A bar where the boy would
eventually spend nights with friends fending off
feelings of inferiority with a few beers and a laugh.
The boy and mom would walk home, arms weighted
with grocery bags. Outside, in a sad city, walking with
his mother, the boy felt safe.

III. SACRED MYSTERY SONGS

"Even your body knows its heritage and its rightful need and will not be deceived. And your body is the harp of your soul, And it is yours to bring forth sweet Music from it or confused sounds."

——KHALIL GIBRAN

ON A COOL NIGHT,
WE PITCHED A TENT.

In the morning the desert makes itself known.
We are forced to wake up
                    before the heat kills us.
We go outside and s   t   r   e   t   c   h our bones and
squint our eyes. The sky is   & blue.
We walk and kick up dust like wild horses.
When we finally reach   our destination
        float
the arias   in the arid air for days, making the *palm trees*
dance in rhythm. We rest for brief moments.
The sun is setting and you lost something.
Now, the sun is gone and the moon glows dim in the luster of
the flashing lights. There are pyrotechnics,
                        lightning-strikes and fire works.
The night is bright and though I can no longer see you, my
eyes have adjusted just fine.

THE ADMIRER IS ADMIRED

it is admirable
that the admired
would admit to
the admirer
amidst the muck
and mire of
a love expired
that the admiration
is mutual

among a multitude
of almost enamored
"I am still here.
Might I admire you
everyday?" asked the admirer.
The admired, in reply,
"Although I'm attracted,
I'm not convinced entirely."
"Might we jump over fire
And grow like lentils?"

Writing amorous epigrams
on the backs of our hands
In love with the scent of rain wetting asphalt.

Writing homespun confessions
on the backs of our hands
In love with me loving you.

HARVEST MOON KISS

The bottom of his Vans sneakers
still sticky with tree sap.

Bits of a haystack stuck.
Cornhusks crunched
as they walked

hidden under a Harvest Moon.
Held hands in an
autumnal haunt.

Carnivalesque
cotton candy, candy apples,
dizzied on a carousel.

Perfectly poised
anxious adolescence
awkwardly rode the Ferris wheel.

Fell fancy-free,
fragile leaves, yellow
like the small glow

of candles in carved pumpkins, hollow.
Kept out the cold in poorly-knit sweaters
hoping the little flame lingered, he whispered:

"I want to kiss you."

VIRGINITY

In ninth grade
I watched *American Pie*,
waiting to taste it.

In eleventh grade
I read *Springs Awakening*.
It was May.

Coming of age.
Coming in pants.
Coming together

    with another body
        for the first time.
She stole my virginity in the spring

    of my eighteenth year.
I stole her heart and
    misplaced it.

    It eventually melted
        some six years later
    and dripped sweet, salty

right through my unfaithful finger tips.
        When the weather permits,
    I swim in nostalgia,

        sinking to the bottom of my heart—
Reenacting the time
    of my virgin suicide.

A FLOWER BLOOMS IN VIRGINIA (NAOMI MARIE)

Somewhere in Virginia,
A flower is blooming.

Somewhere near the beach,
Deep inside the iris,

An overture overseas:
A seed in the soil.

Brought about by U.S. army
brats in Germany.

A Blackipino;
A spitting image of

Modern intimacy.
Different roots offshoot.

At the edge of a petal, love waits.
Extended arms, tiny fingers reach out

To feel the sunlight
Radiate into her radiance.

As she sings sweet syllables
From deep down in her diaphragm,

The peace that exists at the out-breath
Is the name you will maintain.

And you, little bud,
Will always be enough.

O me! You will lead a brilliant life.

LOVE IN A SHOPPING AISLE

I've seen love in a shopping aisle.

A Black man
in the middle of his age.

Pushes his wife in a wheelchair.

The love of his life
suffers some sickness, unfair.

From the sound of her voice
dysarthria has changed her.

Not the woman she once was but
he still loves her like the first time.

"I think the dish soap is in the laundry aisle,"
she said with a slight slur.

"Oh, okay," as he pushes his lover
around the corner.

There exists love in a shopping aisle.

Two women
walk along the freezer section.

One holds the hand-basket, the other rushes ahead.

"Where the fuck do they put the sweetener?"
"Relax, love."

One tells the other
as she reaches for her hand

and rubs her thumb
against the pocket of skin

between the index
and the thumb.

How easy is it to find yourself in love in a shopping aisle?

IV. ENDNOTES

BUILD:

Paragraph 1:
Reference to "Soul Meets Body"
Death Cab For Cutie
Plans (2005),
All We Love We Leave Behind (2012) by Converge.

Paragraph 2:
Inspired by Conrad's *Heart of Darkness (1899)*.
Reference to George A. Romero films.
Reference to "Barbarism Begins At Home"
The Smiths, *Meat is Murder* (1985).
The idea of "doubleness"
Doubles literature:
Nabokov's *Despair* (1965), Saramago's *The Double* (2002),
Conrad's *The Secret Sharer* (1909), *Tales of E.T.A. Hoffmann*
(1972), Dostoevsky's *The Double* (1846),
St. Petersburg tales by Nikolai Gogol,
Stevenson's *Strange Case of Dr. Jekyll and Mr. Hyde* (1886).

Paragraph 3:
Inspired by Sigmund Freud and Jacques Lacan.
Reference to "Floating Spit"
Perfume Genius
Put Your Back N 2 It (2012).
"Beautiful organ donor weather"
dialogue from the TV show, *House M.D.*
The idea of somnambulism
sleepwalking, the zombie-like state
of characters in the horror film,
I Walked With a Zombie (1943)
or the novel, *Kiss of the Spider-Woman* (1976) by Miguel Puig.
The Santo and Johnny song,
"Sleep Walk" (1959), covered by Carlos Santana
for the *La Bamba* (1987) soundtrack.
"Sleepwalking"
The Raveonettes
Pretty in Black (2005).

The idea of destruction
in the final line inspired by
"Imitation is the Sincerest Form of Battery"
Every Time I Die, *The Big Dirty* (2007).

WITHOUT LANGUAGE:
Stanza 3: inspired by
"No Church in the Wild"
Jay-Z, Kanye West, and Frank Ocean
Watch The Throne (2011).

Stanza 6:
inspired by "TOJ" by El-P,
Fantastic Damage (2002).

SCAREHEAD:
Title: "Headlines" Neon Blonde
Chandelier in the Savanna (2005).

Stanza 2, line 1:
Reference to Laura Palmer,
the character murdered
in Twin Peaks (1990).

Stanza 2, line 3:
"I Am a God"
Kanye West.
Yeezus.
Def Jam Recordings, 2013.

Stanza 3, line 2:
Heisenberg, the alter ego
of Walter White
in *Breaking Bad*.

Stanza 8: See Karrin "Superhead"
Steffans' memoir,
Confessions of a Video Vixen (2005).

Stanza 9:
The Walking Dead
and the virus trope in zombie movies.
The idea of outbreaks;
technological illnesses (computer viruses),
chemical warfare and STDs.

INSTITUTIONS OF FUCKERY (LIST INCOMPLETE):
<u>Title</u>: the term "fuckery" is
in "Me and Mr. Jones"
Amy Winehouse
Back to Black (2006).

<u>Line 7</u>: names of various gangs
prominent in Southern California.

<u>Line 18</u>: a hip-hop shock website
featuring viral videos
proliferating stereotypes
of Hip-Hop culture (thereby, Black culture).

REVOLUTIONARY MUSIC (THROUGH A WHITE MALE GAZE):
<u>Stanza 1, line 4</u>: See late 90s rap
videos "Hypnotize" (1997)
The Notorious B.I.G.
"Money Aint A Thang" (1998)
Jay-Z and Jermaine Dupri.

<u>Stanzas 2 & 3</u>: the satirical film,
Bamboozled (2000)
directed by Spike Lee.

<u>Stanza 4, line 2</u>:
"Paint a Vulgar Picture"
The Smiths
Strangeways, Here We Come (1987).

<u>Stanza 4, lines 3 & 4</u>:
"Somewhere in America"
Jay-Z, *Magna Carta...*
Holy Grail (2013).
Twerking:
hip-hop dance move
massively appropriated
by white girls
across America
(example: Miley Cyrus).

<u>Stanza 5, lines 3 & 4</u>:
Dialogue from
"Ask a Black Dude"
Paul Mooney
on *Chappelle's Show* (2003).

<u>Stanza 7, line 4</u>:
"Takeover"
by Jay-Z, *The Blueprint* (2001).
"The Bounce"
Jay-Z and Kanye West
The Blueprint 2 (2003).

NANCY CALLAHAN DATES A RAPPER:
<u>Stanza 2, line 1</u>:
"Big Poppa"
The Notorious B.I.G.
Ready to Die (1994).

<u>Stanza 4, line 2</u>:
Maxwell's version (2001)
of Kate Bush's song,
"This Woman's Work" (1987).

<u>Stanza 6, line 4</u>:
inspired by Toni Morrison's novel,
The Bluest Eye (1970).
Their Eyes Were Watching God (1937)
Zora Neale Hurston.

<u>Stanza 7, line 2</u>:
Nancy Callahan is a principal character
in Frank Miller and Robert Rodriguez's film
Sin City (2005) often critiqued as
anti-feminine and misogynistic.

CLOSE YOUR EYES (BLINK):
<u>Blink 11, stanza 2, line 4</u>: "The Hours"
Beach House, *Bloom* (2012).

NOTHING:
<u>Stanza 3, line 1</u>:
"La Vie En Rose" (1947) by Edith Piaf
used in Oliver Stone's *Natural Born Killers* (1994)
Spike Lee's *Summer of Sam (S.O.S.)* (1999).
The Belgian film, *Ma Vie en rose* (1997),
Ludovic, a transgendered child
seen by her family as a boy.

<u>Stanza 3, line 5</u>:
The Boondock Saints (1999),
The Brothers MacManus place pennies
over the eyes of their victims.
The Pale Man
in Guillermo Del Toro's
Pan's Labyrinth (2006).
The character Sheldon Sands,
played by Johnny Depp,
has his eyes drilled out in
Robert Rodriguez's
Once Upon A Time in Mexico (2003).

THE MEANING OF A GNAT:
Stanza 2, line 3:
"The Boy With The Thorn in His Side"
The Smiths, *The Queen is Dead* (1986).

ENNUI:
Title: Edward Gorey's abecedarian book,
The Gashlycrumb Tinies (1963),
"N is for Neville who died of ennui."

I TURNED ON THE TELEVANGELISM:
Stanza 1, line 4: Trinity Broadcasting Network
Stanza 2, line 1: televangelist, Jan Crouch

HIGH ON RECYCLED AIR:
Line 17: "Nightmare at 200,000 Feet", an episode of *The Twilight Zone* (1963).
Line 23: *Donnie Darko* (2001), deals with paranoia, schizophrenia and time travel.
Line 26: "Recycled Air" by the Postal Service from the album, *Give Up* (2003).

A GUIDE TO SURVIVING THREE DAYS IN THE DESERT:
Stanza 4, line 1:
The Haus of Gaga a creative collective
akin to Andy Warhol's The Factory.
"The House of the Rising Sun" (1964),
The Animals and the cover version
by Lauren O'Connell,
for the television show
American Horror Story: Coven.

Stanza 10, line 3:
Daniel Johnston's song, "Worried Shoes"
covered by Karen O and the Kids
for Spike Jonze's film adapatation
of Maurice Sendak's
Where the Wild Things Are (2009).

<u>Stanza 11, line 2</u>:
"Sheila, Take a Bow"
The Smiths
Louder Than Bombs (1987).

PERFUMED APOCALYPSE:
<u>Stanza 3, line 5</u>:
Black romantic comedy,
Harold and Maude (1971).

<u>Stanza 4, line 5</u>:
"The Archer's Arrows Have Broken"
Brand New, *The Devil and God*
Are Raging Inside Me (2006).

<u>Stanza 4, line 5</u>:
"We Found Love in a Hopeless Place"
Calvin Harris and Rihanna
18 Months (2012).

<u>Stanza 5, line 4</u>:
"Angel lust"
the erect or hardened state
of genital organs
of victims of sudden
and violent deaths
(hanging, gunshot wounds, etc.).
Guy, William A., and Charles A. Lee.
"Death By Hanging." *Principles of Forensic Medicine*.
New York: Harper & Bros., 1845. 245-46. Online.

<u>Stanza 5, line 9</u>:
Poe, Edgar Allan,
and Gary Richard Thompson.
"The Imp of the Perverse."
The Selected Writings of Edgar Allan Poe:
Authoritative Texts, Backgrounds and Contexts, Criticism.
New York: W.W. Norton &, 2004. 402-06.
<u>Stanza 6, line 2</u>: Don DeLillo's *Mao II* (1991).

<u>Stanza 7, line 2</u>: the tagline of David Lynch's
Twin Peaks (1990).

<u>Stanza 8, line 1</u>: *House of Balloons* (2011),
The Weeknd.
A decadent album
concerning escapism
of a young generation
through excessive drug use
and meaningless sex.

<u>Stanza 8, line 4</u>: "Hudson"
Vampire Weekend *Modern Vampires
of the City* (2013).

<u>Stanza 9, line 1</u>: *Reality Bites* (1994).
Juxtaposition of corporeality
and the digital world of information
in the form of bytes.

BROKEN BALLERINA:
<u>Title and content</u> inspired by:
The psychological drama
Black Swan (2010), Darren Aronoksfy.
In the short film,
Runaway (2010), Kanye West
performs the song
accompanied by ballerinas.

<u>Line 16</u>: "Meiple" (pronounced me-I-play)
Robin Thicke and Jay-Z, *Sex Therapy* (2009).
<u>Line 20</u>: "T.O.J." by El-P
Fantastic Damage (2002).

<u>Line 31</u>: *arabesque*
a ballet position.
The dancer stands
on one foot
one arm forward

other arm and leg
held out behind.
Arabesque literature.
Tales of Edgar Allan Poe are
intricate and ornate.

Line 59: passé, the position in ballet
informing the form of this poem—
leg bent upward,
toes toward other leg.
Also, passé, as in
"out of fashion."

NYE**13**:
Line 13: "I Want You"
Elvis Costello, *Blood & Chocolate* (1986).

LITTLE DEATH:
Title and content: French euphemism,
la petite mort, an orgasm.
A spiritual release
post-orgasm, the outflow
after melancholy.
Roland Barthes says
little death is the driving force
for reading literature.

BREAK:
Stanza 2, line 4: *Bloom* (2012)
an album by
Beach house.

ON WEEKENDS:
Stanza 3, lines 2 & 3: "Little Red Corvette" by Prince from *1999*
(1983).
Stanza 8, line 3: "Again" by Janet Jackson from *janet* (1993).

ALIENATED INTELLECTUALS AND SUICIDAL YOUTH:
Stanza 1, line 14: Reference to the film, *Garden State* (2003).

Stanza 2, lines 1 & 2: Felt. "Woman Tonight."
Felt 2: A Tribute to Lisa Bonet.
Rhymesayers Entertainment, 2005.

Stanza 2, line 6: Théophile Gautier's short story,
"The Beautiful Vampire" (1836).
Stanza 2, lines 9 & 10: The Smiths.
"You Just Haven't Earned It Yet, Baby."
The World Won't Listen.
Rough Trade Records, 1987.

Stanza 2, line 12: Inspired by "On"
Bloc Party, *Weekend in the City* (2007).
Stanza 3, line 4: *Roadkill Overcoat* (2007) by Busdriver.

IT HAPPENS ALL THE TIME:
Stanza 1, line 5: Milgram experiment:
Milgram, Stanley. "Behavioral Study of obedience."
The Journal of Abnormal and Social Psychology, Vol 67(4), Oct
1963, 371-378.
Stanza 1, line 6: Tegan and Sara
"Shock To Your System"
Heartthrob (2013).

Stanza 2: inspired by:
Freudian and Jungian
interpretations of teeth dreams:
http://www.teethfallingoutdream.org/
Filipino folklore says a dream about
teeth falling out equates
to the loss of a loved one
(i.e. death):
Zaide, Sonia M.
The Philippines: A Unique Nation.
Quezon City, Philippines: All-Nations Pub., 1999.

EMILY WAS THE BROKEN ONE:
Stanza 5, line 1: a song by Brand New,
from the album *Deja Entendu* (2003).
Stanza 5, line 2: a song by Foo Fighters,
from the album *The Colour and the Shape* (1997).

MOZ KNOWS:
Title:
"I Know It's Over"
The Smiths
The Queen is Dead (1986).

Stanza 1, line 1:
Morrissey is
a prolific British songwriter,
former lead singer of
The Smiths.

Stanza 1, line 4:
"This Charming Man"
The Smiths
The Smiths (1984).

Stanza 2, line 4:
"The Boy With the Thorn in His Side"
The Smiths
The Queen Is Dead (1985).

Stanza 3, line 4:
The Smiths.
"Please, Please, Please,
Let Me Get What I Want".
Hatful of Hollow.
WEA, 1984.

Stanza 4, line 4:
"Hairdresser On Fire"
Morrissey, *Viva Hate* (1988).

AN EXORCISM:
Stanza 4, lines 2 & 3:
"Doo-Wop in the Desert"
A 1950s and1960s themed
Valentine's Day dance
held at the Ace Hotel
in Palm Springs.

Stanza 4, line 5:
The ambiguous final shot
of Stanley Kubrick's, *The Shining* (1980).
An allusion to ghosts
Jack in an old photograph
of the Overlook Hotel,
dressed in 1920s fashion.

YELLOW BUG:
Stanza 7, line 3:
"I Wanna Be Your Dog"
Iggy and The Stooges
The Stooges (1969).
"Dog" by Wavves,
Afraid of Heights (2013).

ON A COOL NIGHT WE PITCHED A TENT.:
Line 5: "Wild Horses"
Atmosphere, *When Life Gives You Lemons,*
You Paint that Shit Gold (2008).
Line 12: "Flashing Lights",
Kanye West, *Graduation* (2007).

Lines 13 & 14: "All of the Lights"
Kanye West, *My Beautiful Dark Twisted Fanstasy* (2010).

THE ADMIRER IS ADMIRED:
Stanza 2, lines 9 & 10: traditions in Persian New Year.

HARVEST MOON KISS:
Stanza 7, line 2:
"In a Sweater, Poorly-knit"
MewithoutYou, *Brother, Sister* (2006).
Stanza 8, line 19:
"Under a Honeymoon"
The Good Life, *Album of the Year* (2004).

VIRGINITY:
Stanza 1, line 2:
The film *American Pie* (1999)
the loss of virginity.

Stanza 2, line 2:
The coming-of-age play,
Springs Awakening (1906)
German dramatist, Frank Wedekind.

Stanza 7, line 3:
"Swim Good" by Frank Ocean,
Nostalgia, ULTRA (2011).

Stanza 8, line 3:
The film *Virgin Suicides* (1999)
Sophia Coppola.

A FLOWER BLOOMS IN VIRGINIA (NAOMI MARIE):
Stanza 6, line 1:
"This Modern Love"
Bloc Party, *Silent Alarm* (2006).

AUTHOR'S NOTE

In the 21st century, we have the luxury of writing our narratives in a multiplicity of ways. As we untangle the webs of our lives, we struggle to construct, deconstruct, and re-construct identity to find meaning in a world split between corporeality and virtual reality. Technology becomes a frenemy—there is a comfortable tension between the human voice and the digital identities we forge in cyberspace. Technology continues to reshape the way we create art and identity, no matter the medium. Even if a poem is not born digital, the urban poet is informed by technology: the Internet and social media, word processing and the process of typing. Millennials and their successors have the past at their fingertips—no longer needing to visit an independent/art house theater or a record shop, the 21st century poet has the technological prowess to appropriate pop culture from the past at the click of a button. With all of this in mind, I have come to look at my poetry in terms of the process rather than the product. The product is often polyphonic and polysemous; many voices and meanings from poem to poem, stanza to stanza, and even line to line. I attribute the multi-vocality of my poems, what I refer to as "remyths" (a portmanteau of "remix" and "myth"), to the "cut-copy-paste" process engrained in the process of typing.

At the cultural moment in which this collection was written (the early 2010s), what I might call "The Era of the Mash-Up,"—a time when music was heavily influenced by Danger Mouse's controversial 2004 *Grey Album*—it became clear to me that the way we invent our own narratives is rooted in the art of sampling; it is something akin to looping a sound bite from a dusty jazz record in a rap song. Poetry fits into a lineage of remixing culture to accommodate our understanding of the world and our place in it. Aside from music—button-mashing DJs that blend any and all genres into one cohesive suite of electronic music—poetry is an art form that lends itself well to the high-speed Internet culture in which we currently live, as the poet Molly Peacock explains in her book, *How to Read a Poem...and Start a Poetry Circle*:

> In a cybermoment when quickness is everything (and it is nice to remember that to quicken means to enliven, that the Book of Common Prayer calls the living "the quick"), poetry, the screen-size art, provides depth. It is both brief and profound. Our hunger is for levels of meaning but our need is instant. Poetry is the art that offers depth in a moment, using the depth of the moment. When a poem fits on a mental screen, then a thought can pierce our busyness. Intensity is our luxury now, not the time it took, say, a hundred years ago, to swim the backstroke through a long, long novel. At this technomoment we must plunge, and poetry offers the deep, quick pool. (13)

Remyth has the ability to insert the private voice of the poet into a conversation with any and every other artist they choose. It creates an instant snapshot full of cultural context, like taking a photo on a camera phone and putting a vintage filter on it, combining the old (art that informs the poet) and new (the voice of the poet) to make new meaning (the remyth).

Remyth is a method of poetry used for healing and reconciliation, be it with the self, romantically, familial, or race and gender relations, by appropriating cultural residue that has stained the mind (i.e. lyrics, films, literature, and television). Often, these moments of popular culture maintain a significant and nostalgic value in relation to one's memory, inextricably linked with a particular abject-noun (a person, place, or thing, living or dead). These residues tend to have a tragic, haunting quality after loss, but by creating a "remyth" we reclaim power over the residual art, allowing for new narratives to come to fruition and, thereby, a remixed identity. "An Exorcism," a poem I wrote about ridding one's self of material possessions that are reminders of an ex-lover, reflects the notion of remyth is a ritual for reconciliation. This healing technique also questions the role of the digital world in how we process trauma and human relations and questions intellectual properties—who owns art, the artist or the consumer? In his book, *Reality Hunger: A Manifesto*,

David Shields takes quotations from various authors, poets, critics, musicians, film makers, and the like, and cuts and pastes them together seamlessly, without letting his reader know who is saying what. This creates a conversation among anonymous voices on the state of American culture, which is both fruitful and chaotic. It leaves the reader with a bulk of cultural images that possess iconic value within an American historical context. Don DeLillo's 1991 novel, *Mao II*, speaks to the notion of the mass-production of images and its effect on culture as a whole. Two decades later, the proliferation of images and pastiche is at an all-time high and as Andy Warhol once said:

> Everybody has their own America, and then they have pieces of a fantasy America that they think is out there but they can't see [...] so the fantasy corners of America [...] you've pieced them together from scenes in movies and music and lines from books. And you live in your dream America that you've custom-made from art and schmaltz and emotions just as much as you live in your real one. (*America*, 8)

One quotation in *Reality Hunger* that speaks to my idea of remyth poetry states, "the citation of sources belongs to the realms of journalism and scholarship, not art [...] what counts are the ways in which these common copies of creative work can be linked, manipulated, tagged, highlighted, bookmarked, translated, enlivened by other media, and sewn together in the universal library" (29-30). Much of the content of my poetry is steeped in appropriation and the stitching together of moments in pop culture in order to make sense of the zeitgeist and historical context in which we are living. For example, in a poem like "Scarehead" I attempt to capture many voices of sensationalized events that occurred in the past two decades in order to understand America's obsession with romanticizing or mythologizing realities. To do this, it really is a matter of copying, pasting, and juxtaposing voices in a cohesive or confusing manner, depending on the intention I have for a given poem.

I also take into account the physical conditions of my

writing process, which is very rhythmic and intuitive. I listen to music and apply a method of cut and paste, in which I have a Word document open with pages of ideas for lines that I have collected over the years. I follow the rhythm of the music, which ranges from aggressive, to sensual, to cerebral, and mix and match lines according to what each song makes me feel. For example, I wrote the poem, "Alienated Intellectuals and Suicidal Youth" while listening to "No Love," an aggressively chaotic song by Death Grips, whereas with the poem, "Harvest Moon Kiss," I was listening to "Lover's Rock" by Sade. The sharp tones of certain poems or the languid, sensual ambiance of others is dictated by my bodily rhythm.

This physical aspect of my poetry is in accordance with Robert Pinsky's idea of poetry as bodily. In his book *The Sounds of Poetry: A Brief Guide*, he explains,

> The technology of poetry, using the human body as its medium, evolved for specific uses: to hold things in memory, both within and beyond the individual life span; to achieve intensity and sensual appeal; to express feelings and ideas rapidly and memorably. To share those feelings and ideas with companions, and also with the dead and with those to come after us. (9)

As my work rests in the realm of free verse and I tend not to follow any specific meters, I am very interested in the sound of poetry. As Peacock states, "how the poem feels to your tongue and teeth—the consonants, the vowels, the loudness and softness of syllables—is the embodiment of the feelings that sounds evoke" (28). For me, a poem can be meticulously written on the page; it can have perfect iambic pentameter, precise grammatical line breaks, bloated poetic language, or other interesting manipulations visually, but if the sound does not capture me, I fail to find depth in it. It is the invisible sound that captures me first; seeing the syntax on the page comes second. James Longenbach illustrates the importance of sound in poetry, as he states in his book *The Art of the Poetic Line*, "poems are poems because we want to listen to them. Some poems have a prominent argument; some poems don't. But all poems live or die on their capacity to lure us

from their beginnings to their ends by patter of sounds"
(120). In poems such as "On a cool night, we pitched a tent."
or "Dresser Drawers," I play with the words on the page a lot
more than other poems, but the listener would not be moved
by these manipulations were it not for my use of alliteration.
I agree with Peacock when she explains that "poetry is really
the fusion of three arts: music, story-telling, and painting.
The line displays the poem's music, the sentence displays its
thoughts, and the image displays the vision of the poet" (19).

Since the act of writing a poem is very physical for me, I
also believe that "reading a poem gives you an almost physical
experience of a mental activity" (Peacock, 14). Much of my
influence comes from the American musician and poet Saul
Williams. I have seen him read, or rather perform, his poetry
from memory, and it was only in hearing it that I became
so hypnotized by the sounds and rhythms that I went and
purchased his poetry books. His book *,said the shotgun to the
head.,* is one 192-page poem filled with interesting syntax and
elements of Dada and Futurist poetic techniques. Having
heard portions of it performed first, it took on a new life
when I looked at the composition, which incorporates the
manipulation of space on the page. This helped me write my
poem, "Little Death," in which I chose to create a circular
shape that resembles a mouth moaning during intercourse, or
any other bodily orifice capable of being penetrated during
sex—it's meant to convey the endlessness of a finite moment
of physicality that teeters between life-affirming and horrific
violence. To read it is dizzying and tiring. I also chose to
create the title by cutting out letters from an old newspaper
and pasting them onto the computer paper much like a
ransom note—this speaks to the psychological meeting the
physical in power, the abuse of power, and the dynamics of
power in sex. It entangles the deliberate announcement into
a spiral into a complicit whisper. Hearing "Little Death" read
aloud is a different experience from seeing it on the page,
where the form matches the violent and chaotic content.
Since there are no period marks or commas, the readers' only
cue is the capital letters. In this way, the syntax helps dictate
the rhythm a reader will vocalize a poem. The most a poet

can do is use syntax and line breaks to give the reader hints as to how to manipulate one's body to match what is written.

A relationship between the poet and the reader becomes physical regardless of the time and space between them. As Pinksy states, "poetry is vocal, which is to say a bodily, art. The medium of poetry is a human body [...] the medium is the audience's body [...] this makes the art physical, intimate, vocal and individual" (8). Writing, editing, and of course, the vocalization of a poem are all very physical processes. This idea is sprinkled throughout my collection, with the notion of body as landscape for the theme of reconciliation. This can be seen in the poem "broken ballerina" and a variety of others in which the body is the focal point. Other poems in this thesis are more cerebral and abstract—out of body and more focused on the thought. These cerebral poems tend to express my use of caesura and other kinds of line breaks.

According to James Longenbach:

> Poetry is the sound of language organized in lines. More than meter, more than rhyme, more than images or alliteration or figurative language, line is what distinguishes our experience of poetry as poetry, rather than some other kind of writing [...] line cannot be understood by describing the line alone: the music of a poem—no matter if metered, syllabic, or free—depends on what the syntax is doing when the line ends. (xi-xii)

In much of my poetry, I like to use caesura because it alludes to the chaos of thought itself. In poems like "broken ballerina," "Break" and "Close Your Eyes (Blink)," lines are incredibly fractured, often in the middle of a sentence, in order to create a disconnect and a syncopated rhythm that I perceive the brain and heart to have at moments of sheer panic or anxiety. At these moments in life, thoughts do not come in neatly constructed sentences—they come in fragments that, only in retrospection, can we assemble into cohesive lines.

Another technique I use in my poetry is couplets, seen in "Love in a Shopping Aisle." In both the poems with frenetic line breaks and the ones using more uniform couplets, tercets and quatrains, form matches the content. If I am ruminating on a storm of thoughts that enter my mind as my airplane ascends into the sky, as I do in "High on Recycled Air," I use many fragmented line breaks to emphasize the panic in that specific moment, as many tragic scenarios that I am helpless to control flash through my mind and in turn, the readers'. In "Love in a Shopping Aisle," I use couplets to symbolize the intimacy and inseparability of two people in love. These people are connected by the subtleties that have brought them together in the same way the couplets create a union of one cohesive sentence made of two lines.

In addition to these syntactical elements, a noir aspect can be found in my poems, which harkens back to the idea that poetry connects the poet and the reader. The use of "you" and "I" in relation to fast-paced, hard-boiled narration in poems such as "Alienated Intellectuals and Suicidal Youth" or "Close Your Eyes (Blink)" gives the reader a chance to read or hear the poem in a cinematic fashion; it plays out like a scene in which the self is both the detective and the criminal. In such poems, both the poet and the reader are implicated as the mystery to be solved. These poems, along with the prose poems "Genevieve Street" and "Build," have a narrative quality. In the prose poems, I chose to leave out line breaks as homage to authors like Joseph Conrad or Vladimir Nabokov, who possess a poetic language that enriches their prose. In other words, they weave together sentences that not only keep the story moving, but the sentences also sound beautiful. I wanted to apply this same aesthetic to these two poems, which are much more narrative than the others.

Lastly, I have added endnotes to this collection to give greater context and understanding of the poems. The addition of endnotes is to highlight remix culture by taking advantage of the multi-vocal. This is achieved by blending various voices together in order to create new meaning (a remyth). For example, if a poem alludes to a particular song or film, perhaps the reader could read the poem as they listen to the song or after they watch the film that might be referenced. This intertextuality will add another dimension or connection to the content, either intellectually or emotionally. In many cases, the works cited are merely referenced to or were the inspiration for a particular line of a poetry I've written; very seldom are there quotations from other sources and in those cases, I have cited them using all of the attributes necessary for proper MLA citation. I have structured the endnotes to act as smaller companion poems, playing with the traditional structure of proper citation by breaking lines to emphasize the artist, the particular reference (song, film, etc.), and the whole body of work from which it came. This organization of the endnotes speaks to the title of my thesis. A remyth is achieved through the postmodern ritual of creating and negotiating one's identity through voices that are no longer just sources on a Works Cited page, but fragmented samples embedded in the newborn composition that add greatly to the rhythm, tone and syntax of the poetry.

WORKS CITED

Longenbach, James. *The Art of the Poetic Line*. Graywolf, 2008. pp. xi-xii+.
Peacock, Molly. *How to Read a Poem...and Start a Poetry Circle*. Riverhead, 1999, pp. 13-14+.
Pinsky, Robert. *The Sounds of Poetry: A Brief Guide*, Farrar, Straus and Giroux, 1998, pp. 8-9.
Shields, David. *Reality Hunger: A Manifesto*, Alfred A. Knopf, 2010, pp. 29-30.
Warhol, Andy. *America*, Harper & Row, 1985, p. 8.

ACKNOWLEDGMENTS

Gratitude to my Higher Power—thank You for the vessel, the voice, the guidance of the pen and my fingertips to invoke the thoughts and feelings within my heart and mind.

Thank you, Mom and Dad, for the love and lessons. Thank you for your mistakes and your growth. Thank you for raising me to have a faith and to believe in myself, and for accepting me as a creative being even when our beliefs do not align.

Thank you, Leslie, for helping me understand this collection—no matter how psychically or physically ill it has made me feel over the years—as a spell unwittingly cast nearly a decade ago. Thank you for choosing to read this, and accepting and loving me.

Thank you to my thesis committee at Chapman University, Dr. Anna Leahy, Dr. Karen An-hwei Lee, and Tom Zoellner, and my graduate school colleagues and friends for the feedback and support.

Thank you to Cati Porter and Inlandia Institute for finding the beauty and utility in my words. It's surreal to know you've taken my manuscript in and given it a home. I will forever treasure this collaboration.

Adam Daniel Martinez first scraped his knee playing in his hometown of San Bernardino, California. Since then, as a first-generation Chicano college student, he has earned a dual MA/MFA in English and Creative Writing at Chapman University. Adam has written and performed music in the Inland Empire for over 15 years, most notably under the moniker Faimkills. He is the co-founder of *Pour Vida*, a digital literary zine. Currently, Adam enjoys sharing his love for words with his students as an English professor at Chaffey College. He lives in Redlands, California with his wife and two cats, Virginia and Percival.

ABOUT THE HILLARY GRAVENDYK PRIZE

The Hillary Gravendyk Prize is an open poetry book competition published by Inlandia Institute for all writers regardless of the number of previously published poetry collections.

HILLARY GRAVENDYK (1979-2014) was a beloved poet living and teaching in Southern California's "Inland Empire" region. She wrote the acclaimed poetry book, *HARM* from Omnidawn Publishing (2012), the posthumously published *The Soluble Hour* (Omnidawn, 2017), *Unlikely Conditions* (1913 Press, 2017, with Cynthia Arrieu-King), as well as the poetry chapbook *The Naturalist* (Achiote Press, 2008). A native of Washington State, she was an admired Assistant Professor of English at Pomona College in Claremont, CA. Her poetry has appeared widely in journals such as *American Letters & Commentary, The Bellingham Review, The Colorado Review, The Eleventh Muse, Fourteen Hills, MARY, 1913: A Journal of Forms, Octopus Magazine, Tarpaulin Sky* and *Sugar House Review.* She was awarded a 2015 Pushcart Prize for her poem "Your Ghost," which appeared in the Pushcart Prize Anthology. She leaves behind many devoted colleagues, friends, family and beautiful poems. Hillary Gravendyk passed away on May 10, 2014 after a long illness. This contest has been established in her memory.

ABOUT INLANDIA INSTITUTE

Inlandia Institute is a regional non-profit and literary center. We seek to bring focus to the richness of the literary enterprise that has existed in this region for ages. The mission of the Inlandia Institute is to recognize, support, and expand literary activity in all of its forms in Inland Southern California by publishing books and sponsoring programs that deepen people's awareness, understanding, and appreciation of this unique, complex and creatively vibrant region.

The Institute publishes books, presents free public literary and cultural programming, provides in-school and after school enrichment programs for children and youth, holds free creative writing workshops for teens and adults, and boot camp intensives. In addition, every two years, the Inlandia Institute appoints a distinguished jury panel from outside of the region to name an Inlandia Literary Laureate who serves as an ambassador for the Inlandia Institute, promoting literature, creative literacy, and community. Laureates to date include Susan Straight (2010-2012), Gayle Brandeis (2012-2014), Juan Delgado (2014-2016), Nikia Chaney (2016-2018), and Rachelle Cruz (2018-2020).

To learn more about the Inlandia Institute, please visit our website at www.InlandiaInstitute.org.

OTHER HILLARY GRAVENDYK PRIZE BOOKS

The Silk the Moths Ignore by Bronwen Tate
Winner of the 2019 National Hillary Gravendyk Prize

Former Possessions of the Spanish Empire by Michelle Peñaloza
Winner of the 2018 National Hillary Gravendyk Prize

All the Emergency-Type Structures by Elizabeth Cantwell
Winner of the 2018 Regional Hillary Gravendyk Prize

Our Bruises Kept Singing Purple by Malcolm Friend
Winner of the 2017 National Hillary Gravendyk Prize

Traces of a Fifth Column by Marco Maisto
Winner of the 2016 National Hillary Gravendyk Prize

God's Will for Monsters by Rachelle Cruz
Winner of the 2016 Regional Hillary Gravendyk Prize
Winner of a 2018 American Book Award

Map of an Onion by Kenji C. Liu
Winner of the 2015 National Hillary Gravendyk Prize

All Things Lose Thousands of Times by Angela Peñaredondo
Winner of the 2015 Regional Hillary Gravendyk Prize